OKANAGAN COLLEGE LIBRARY

03513801

D1616917

The Expansion of Tolerance

OKANAGAN COLLEGE
LIBRARY
BRITISH COLUMBIA

The Expansion of Tolerance

Religion in Dutch Brazil
(1624-1654)

Jonathan Israel and Stuart B. Schwartz
Introduction by Michiel van Groesen

AMSTERDAM UNIVERSITY PRESS

Cover design: Kok Korpershoek, Amsterdam

ISBN 978 90 5356 902 3
NUR 686/691

© Amsterdam University Press, Amsterdam 2007

All rights reserved. Without limiting the rights under copyright reserved above, no part of this book may be reproduced, stored in or introduced into a retrieval system, or transmitted, in any form or by any means (electronic, mechanical, photocopying, recording or otherwise) without the written permission of both the copyright owner and the author of the book.

Table of Contents

Michiel van Groesen

Introduction

Tolerance in the early modern Dutch Republic is a topic that has fascinated generations of scholars, and continues to do so. After decades of merciless laws against religious dissidents under Emperor Charles V (1515-56) and his son King Philip II, and periods of strong persecution, the iconoclastic movement which swept the Low Countries in 1566, and the subsequent Revolt against Spain, altered the religious landscape of the Netherlands. The pluriformity of denominations was acknowledged as a permanent feature of society, while the Union of Utrecht in 1579 famously guaranteed that nobody was to be persecuted or investigated for religious reasons. Although the rebels and their leader – and champion of toleration – William of Orange had to concede the provinces of Flanders and Brabant to the Spanish armies, and hence to Catholicism, in the 1580s, freedom of conscience was eventually established in the seven northern provinces that were to form the Dutch Republic.

The Reformed Church, as it became the dominant religious force in this new and unprecedented political entity, did not acquire the exclusive status previously enjoyed by the Catholic Church. Calvinists only comprised a small minority of the population of the Dutch Republic, and the church was never able to enforce a position analogous to Protestant churches in some territories of the Holy Roman Empire after the Peace of Augsburg. Despite being the official church of the United Provinces, it had to accept freedom of conscience, and to some extent freedom of private worship, for Lutherans, Anabaptists, and even Catholics. Strict Calvinists, while not advocating confessional diversity, were well aware of the limitations of their authority in religious affairs, with many people in the Dutch Republic rejecting their beliefs and their insistence on church discipline.

Tolerance, in the long run, proved to be the best and most pragmatic solution to the problem of religious pluriformity, and, as the seventeenth century progressed, came to be regarded as a political virtue with clear social and, more importantly, economic benefits. After the influx of affluent merchants from the Southern Netherlands in the 1580s and 1590s, a shot in the arm of the economy of the northern provinces, the Dutch Republic remained an attractive haven for refugees of various denominations. Lutherans from Germany and Scandinavia arrived in the 1620s and 1630s, presenting the United Provinces with the cheap workforce it required, while financially powerful Sephardic Jews who flocked to Amsterdam provided an international network as well as significant investments to stimulate Iberian and overseas trade. Finally, Huguenots arrived from France after the revocation of the Edict of Nantes in 1685, facilitating a short-lived recovery of the 'rich trades' and the silk industry.

Yet tolerance, despite its appeal to the religiously persecuted from abroad, was subject to limitations and restrictions. Catholics, long considered potential allies of Spain, were treated as second-rate citizens even after 1648. In the latter half of the century, sectarian groups challenging the divinity of Christ, the Trinity, the immortality of the soul, and the divine authorship of the Scripture entered dangerous territory. Controversial books were either immediately banned, or only deemed suitable by the author for posthumous publication, most famously in the case of Spinoza's main philosophical works, *Ethics* and *Tractatus Theologico-Politicus*. All these measures enabled secular magistrates to pose as the defenders of moral and religious order, conveniently sidestepping possible criticism from the Reformed Church.

Early Dutch overseas expansion, instantly successful after its start in the 1590s, neatly reflected the religious situation at home. Successive Dutch fleets to Asia, controlled from 1602 onwards by the monopolistic Dutch East India Company, pursued exclusively mercantile objectives, carrying trading commodities rather than Reformed settlers, arms rather than missionaries. Unlike the Spanish *Conquistadores* in most parts of the New World, the Dutch encountered powerful, self-confident monarchies across the Orient. Coercion, then, had to go hand in hand with diplomacy. Faced with this situation, the Dutch restricted their geographical expansion to trading posts, and tried to collaborate effectively with indigenous rulers. Nowhere did they display any of the missionary zeal of the Spaniards in the Americas, or the Portuguese in West Africa and parts of the Indian subcontinent.

Engraving in *Reysboeck van het rijcke Brasilien* (1624), showing how the Dutch lacked detailed cartographical and geographical knowledge of Brazil before their conquest of Pernambuco in 1630. It optimistically shows the rich rewards to be expected from the capitanía Pernambuco. In the middle of the composition Recife is depicted (E), to the extreme right is Olinda. The sugar plantation on the left is inspired by Theodore de Bry's engraving of sugar production in Brazil (see the illustration on page 48).

The situation in Brazil was fundamentally different from the equilibrium in Asia. After finally gaining a foothold in north-eastern Brazil in 1630, the Dutch needed a skilled workforce in order to exploit the colony's sugar production. Consequent attempts to lure settlers from the United Provinces and war-ravaged Germany to Brazil, however, had remained largely fruitless, as peasants preferred familiar hardships in Europe over an uncertain future in tropical circumstances. Left with few options, the Dutch West India Company (WIC), founded in 1621 to disturb the Iberian domination of the Americas, turned to the skilful and vastly experienced Luso-Brazilian inhabitants, the *moradores*. Soon their detailed knowledge of the sugar industry was complemented by an imported workforce from across the Atlantic, as the Dutch entered the lucrative international slave trade in the late 1630s.

Governor-General Johan Maurits (r. 1637-44) continued the policy set out by the WIC, and the conquest of Angola in 1641 saw the Dutch slave trade gaining true momentum. More than 20,000 Africans, physically well-equipped to work on the Brazilian sugar plantations, thus added further variation to the already pluriform population of the colony. Moreover, in order to make the return of the *moradores* to the coast more attractive, after most of them had moved inland to escape Dutch-Portuguese hostilities, the Governor-General offered freedom of worship, and implemented judicial reforms. The measures were designed to allow various ethnic groups to live alongside each other, and further strengthened Johan Maurits's own reputation as a humanist and enlightened ruler, which had already been established by a vibrant court-life, and a position as a personal *mecenas* (patron) of art, architecture, and science.

Historiography of the Dutch interlude in Brazil, in both Europe and South America, has tended to emphasize the importance of Johan Maurits's seven-year tenure as Governor-General, for instance José Antônio Gonsalves de Mello's *Tempo dos Flamengos* (1947). A persistent problem, however, is that many of the Brazilian scholarly publications have only appeared in Portuguese, limiting their influence on the international historical debate. Significantly, Gonsalves de Mello's study was only translated into Dutch as recently as 2001. Other landmarks of Brazilian historiography, such as the same author's *Gente da Nação. Cristãos-novos e Judeus em Pernambuco 1542-1654* (1989), about the large Sephardic community in north-eastern Brazil, and Evaldo Cabral de Mello's *Olinda Restaurada: guerra e açúcar no Nordeste, 1630-1654* (1975), dealing with the military side of the Dutch-Portuguese hostilities, have not yet been translated, neither into English nor into Dutch. A recent Dutch translation of Cabral de Mello's *O Negócio do Brasil: Portugal, os Países Baixos e o Nordeste, 1641-1669* (1998) offers hope of greater academic interaction. Published in 2005, *De Braziliaanse affaire: Portugal, de Republiek der Verenigde Nederlanden en Noord-Oost Brazilië, 1641-1669* discusses the diplomatic relations between the Portuguese and the Dutch West India Company.

The single book that has succeeded in bridging the linguistic gap, Charles R. Boxer's classic study *The Dutch in Brazil, 1624-1654*, first published in 1957, therefore remains a pivotal work, comprehensively describing and analyzing the political developments in the colony. In the Netherlands meanwhile, the rise of cultural history as a subdiscipline has seen an increase in awareness of the artistic and scientific achievements of

Johan Maurits's reign, culminating in two large exhibitions in 1979 and 2004 in the 'Mauritshuis', Johan Maurits's former domicile in The Hague. The first initiative was accompanied by a comprehensive volume of essays, *Johan Maurits van Nassau-Siegen 1604-1679*, highlighting various aspects of Dutch Brazil and its Governor-General, while the latter was dedicated to the ethnographical paintings by Albert Eckhout, and thus formed an extension to a recent Brazilian work on Eckhout's colleague Frans Post and his drawings kept in the British Museum.

The only work to focus primarily on the religious situation in Dutch Brazil, and the topic of tolerance, was written by Frans L. Schalkwijk in 1986. Despite its recent translation into English, *The Reformed Church in Dutch Brazil (1630-1654)* (1998) has received relatively little attention in the Netherlands. Schalkwijk, a minister living in Recife for decades, studied both the internal structure of the Reformed Church in Dutch Brazil, and the limited missionary efforts displayed by the Dutch, based on archival material in both Brazil and the Netherlands. He argued that religious toleration in Brazil experienced its zenith under Dutch government. When the Portuguese regained control in 1654, this relative freedom was quickly abolished, and replaced by fierce repression of the indigenous people. The two articles in this volume, by Jonathan Israel and Stuart B. Schwartz, build on Schalkwijk's study, attempting to provide further pieces of the religious puzzle that is Dutch Brazil. Both authors focus on the broadness and the variety of toleration in the north-eastern colony.

Jonathan Israel argues that religious toleration in Dutch Brazil, limited yet at the same time unprecedented on this scale in the seventeenth century, preceded the arrival of Johan Maurits in 1637, and was extended after the Governor-General's return to the Dutch Republic in 1644. It was tolerance in general, rather than the enlightened views of just one man alone, that was crucial to the viability and prosperity of the Brazilian colony. Hence Catholics and Jews were given freedom of conscience and freedom of private worship in accordance with Dutch guidelines. Jews in particular, indispensable for financing the Dutch-Brazilian sugar industry, built up a social and economic position unlike elsewhere in the overseas world or in Europe. The demise of New Holland in 1654 also drew the curtain on Jewish privileges, although Jews continued to enjoy a favoured position in other Dutch colonies in the West.

Stuart B. Schwartz, in his contribution, emphasizes that religious toleration in Dutch Brazil was not exclusively the domain of the Dutch. By using Iberian Inquisitorial documents, he stresses the widespread approval of tolerance at grassroots level, with Spanish and Portuguese planters, soldiers, and even some of the clergy accepting an individual's preference to follow his own path to salvation. This liberal attitude towards the individual experience of religion was transferred to Portuguese Brazil, resulting in interconfessional friendships and even marriages in the period when the Dutch controlled the colony. The importance of sugar for the prosperity of Pernambuco required constant interaction between the Dutch, the Portuguese, and the native population, and this co-operation rather than their various backgrounds determined their identities. Even Johan Maurits, himself a zealous Calvinist, had close connections with several Catholic priests.

Both articles presented here were first delivered as papers at the 'Dutch Brazil' symposium held in June 2004 at the Universiteit van Amsterdam, in commemoration of both the fourth centenary of Johan Maurits's birth, and the 350th anniversary of the end of Dutch rule in Brazil. Both authors extensively revised their papers for publication. The conference was organised by the Centre for Latin American Research and Documentation (CEDLA) and the Amsterdam Centre for the Study of the Golden Age, and their efforts were once again combined to prepare this publication.

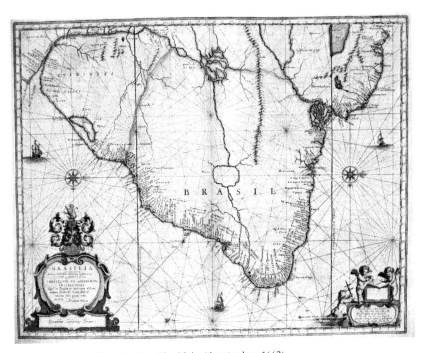

Joan Blaeu, Map of Brazil in his *Atlas Maior* (Amsterdam 1662).

Jonathan Israel

Religious Toleration in Dutch Brazil (1624-1654)

Given that 'toleration' more than any other single aspect is what gives Dutch history its European, wider western, and general world significance, Dutch Brazil between 1624 and 1654 arguably has a special place in the history of the Old and New Worlds and in the history of modern secular society. But while it is legitimate to emphasize – and celebrate – the remarkable degree of religious toleration established under Dutch rule in north-eastern Brazil between the taking of Recife and Olinda, in 1630, and the final surrender of the remaining Dutch enclaves to the Portuguese crown, towards the end of the First Anglo-Dutch War in 1654, it is also important, for the sake of historical accuracy, and our awareness of the making of 'modernity', to avoid the tendency to oversimplification and an overoptimistic assessment which often attends public discussion of exceptional historical phenomena of this sort.

   Although the comparative toleration instituted by the Dutch West India Company (WIC) in its South American colony did diverge dramatically from the main lines of Spanish and Portuguese social governance and regulation as practiced throughout the rest of Ibero-America both before and after the brief 'Dutch' interlude in Brazil, it is necessary to bear in mind that this never amounted to a comprehensive, principled freedom of religion and expression based on any conception of individual freedom in matters of conscience and lifestyle. In fact, what the story of Dutch Brazil, and the limitations and weaknesses of its toleration, really teaches, it might fairly be said, is the impossibility of basing a stable and lasting toleration on the kind of purely pragmatic premises and considerations which applied in the Atlantic world during the era of the Thirty Years' War; and also the relevance, for the historian and students of history, of acquiring a firm and detailed appreciation of the emphatically philosophical character of the 'toleration' which eventually did transform Western society, beginning with the theories of Spinoza, Bayle, and Locke in the late seventeenth century.

Despite its impressive resonance in retrospect, for us today, the tolerance practiced in north-eastern Brazil under Dutch occupation seems to have had very little, if any, symbolic significance either for the late seventeenth century European toleration debate where this topic, seemingly, is virtually never mentioned or indeed for the Enlightenment proper. The great encyclopaedias of the eighteenth century have little to say about the Dutch Brazilian episode and where it is referred to, as for instance in Zedler's *Universal-Lexicon*, published in sixty-four volumes in the 1730s and 1740s, we learn only that the Dutch had established themselves in part of Brazil, and strongly for a time, 'vornehmlich unter Anführung Graf Moritzens von Nassau [...] aber kaum war er weg' – he left in May 1644 – 'so empörte sich das Land, worinnen die Holländer zu ihren Schaden allzuviel Portugiesen hatten wohnen lassen' – hardly a recommendation for toleration.

It is doubtless true, as several historians stress, that the traditions of the House of Oranje-Nassau, and the particular courtly Neo-Stoic values cultivated in Johan Maurits's own personal circle, as well as his bitter experiences during the 1620s when he saw his native principality of Nassau-Siegen occupied by pro-Habsburg forces, and a formal persecution of the local Calvinist communities instigated, powerfully reinforced his instinctive commitment to toleration and a co-existence of churches.[1] Yet however pivotal his own personal role during the seven and a fraction years he spent as the West India Company's Governor-General of Dutch Brazil from January 1637 to May 1644, we should avoid the habit, to which some of the literature on Dutch Brazil is prone, of attributing much, or most, of what was achieved in respect to toleration to his own personal benevolence, prudence and good sense. For quite apart from the fact he had to work within the harsh political realities of the Iberian New World of his time, and the mental framework of relentless confessional conflict then so preponderant in Germany and the Low Countries, he was obliged also to work within guide-lines laid down for him by the directors of the WIC; a joint-stock commercial enterprise, certainly, but also a political and military organization headed by a board of directors and loosely supervised in The Hague by the States General, and through the latter by the States of Holland and Zeeland.

Theodore Matham, Engraved portrait of Johan Maurits of Nassau-Siegen, published in Caspar Barlaeus's *Rerum per octennium in Brasilia* (Amsterdam 1647).
Barlaeus composed the laudatory poem below the portrait.

HISTORIE
Ofte

Iaerlijck Verhael
Uan de
Berrichtinghen der Geoctroyeerde

Weſt-Indiſche Compagnie,

Zedert haer Begin / tot het eynde van 't jaer
ſeſthien-hondert ſes-en-dertich;

Begrepen in Derthien Boecken,

Ende met verſcheyden koperen Platen verciert:

Beſchreven door

IOANNES DE LAET
Bewint-hebber der ſelver Compagnie.

TOT LEYDEN,

By Bonaventuer ende Abraham Elſevier, ANNO 1644.

Met Privilegie.

Title page of Johannes de Laet's *Historie ofte Iaerlijck Verhael* (Leiden 1644).

The governing body of the WIC, the Heren XIX, in fact drew up an agreed set of political ordinances for the governance of all its conquests in the New World, in October 1629, in which it laid down that the Dutch Reformed Church, organized on the same basis as the Reformed Church in the United Provinces, would be the sole and exclusive public church in all its territories; and hence the only ecclesiastical body to be linked with the administration, army, navy, and judiciary, and the confession to which all its commanders and higher office-holders were expected to adhere. At the same time, though, certain specific proposals for religious toleration were instituted.[2] Since in their strategic deliberations of the 1620s, as recounted among others by the chronicler De Laet, as also in their published propaganda and publicity designed to drum up support and investment for the Company, the directors had always made much of the allegedly cruel exploitation of various oppressed peoples and groups reportedly suffering under Spanish and Portuguese colonial rule – especially native peoples and the New Christian descendants of former forcibly baptized Jews – predicting that these groups would eagerly and whole-heartedly support the Dutch in any attempts that they made to wrest Ibero-American territories from Iberian hands, it is not surprising to find that the directors from the outset intended to make provision to secure a good understanding, and military alliances, with native American populations and to attract New Christian and Sephardic Jewish settlement by according this group freedom to practice their religion undisturbed in private homes. Whether or not this aspect of their calculations rested more on fantasy than a realistic appraisal of circumstances, it is striking that, during the 1620s at least, the Spanish royal *Consejo de Estado* (Council of State) in Madrid showed definite signs of alarm at the possibility that New Christians scattered across many parts of the Spanish and Portuguese empires might defect both from the Iberian crowns and the Catholic faith and flock to join the Dutch.[3]

OLINDA

Claes Jansz. Visscher, *View of Pernambuco* (1630). This detail shows Olinda, the Portuguese capital of Pernambuco, just after it has been conquered by Admiral Hendrick Loncq. The Portuguese religious infrastructure is still visible, with the Sao Francisco Church prominently depicted in the middle. On the right, behind the second large church, is the tower of the Jesuit Church.

Clearly, it was never the intention to drive out the Iberian Catholic colonists and planters, or their black and mixed-race slaves and servants, but rather reconcile these as best they could to the prospect of Dutch rule – unrealistic in the long term though this may have been.[4] Accordingly, the 1629 ordinances, while by no means wholly abandoning the Calvinist zeal and hostility to Catholic 'superstition' figuring so prominently in the Company's early propaganda in the Netherlands,[5] included an article directing WIC commanders to accord liberty of conscience, as it is expressed, to the 'Spaniards, Portuguese, and natives of the land, whether they be Roman Catholics or Jews'.[6] However, this was not regarded as a right, or a necessarily permanent privilege, but merely a political concession to two particular groups, a privilege deemed strategically advantageous to the Company. The same clause also stipulates that this freedom of religion should not be limited to private practice, as was then often the case in northern Europe, but should extend also to freedom of 'exercise' of both the Catholic and Jewish faiths; implying, albeit nothing explicit was said about this, that the presence of ordained priests and rabbis on Dutch-controlled territory would be permitted. The one clear prohibition included at this juncture was Article 11 of the ordinances, stipulating the exclusion of the Jesuits and other members of Catholic religious orders. If the Catholic

Frans Post, *View of Olinda* (1662). Post emphasizes the ruinous state of the former capital, which he may have witnessed during his stay in Brazil, as the stones of buildings in Olinda were being used by the Dutch to build Recife and Mauricia.

churches and monasteries of Olinda were pillaged and burnt during the course of the invasion of north-eastern Brazil from 1630 to 1632, most Catholic foundations in the area overrun by the Dutch were preserved and their integrity respected, even though a majority of the friars, and many priests, actually fled the area under Dutch control. Hence, Catholic worship, like Indian freedom, as decreed by the directors was firmly established in Brazil well before Johan Maurits's arrival on the scene. The edict of the Heren XIX of 1635, expelling the remaining friars and Jesuits from Dutch Brazil a year before the count's arrival, was therefore not part of any denial of religious toleration but simply a more precise implementation of the rules laid down by the Company in 1629, and restated in the terms of surrender under which Pernambuco, in 1630, and Paraíba, in 1634, submitted to the Dutch.

A policy of pragmatic co-existence increasingly took hold. After 1636, a number of Portuguese were permitted to live in the inner township of Recife (Pernambuco) alongside the Dutch and Jews. Yet the toleration accorded to the Catholics was inevitably circumscribed in various ways, given the circumstances of the struggle between the Dutch and the Iberian crowns. Among the more restrictive measures were prohibitions on instituting a bishop in the territory under the Dutch and on all correspondence of

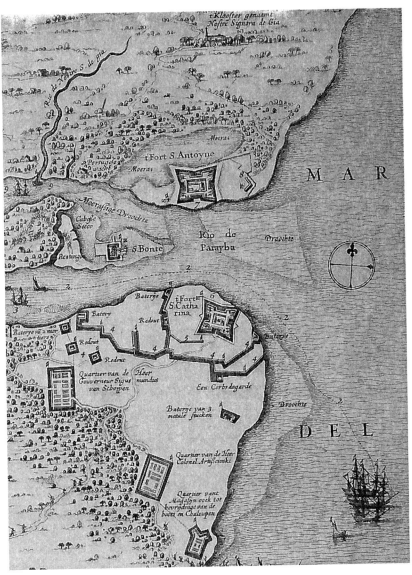

Claes Jansz. Visscher, *Map of Paraíba* (1634, detail). This part of the engraving shows the harbour of Paraíba, or Frederikstad under the rule of the Dutch, with its forts.

Catholics in the Dutch zone with the bishop of Bahia, the nearest major stronghold in the Portuguese zone of Brazil; the consequence of which was to deny the Catholic community under the Dutch all access to episcopal guidance and authority in social as in theological matters, and heighten the effect of the lack of Catholic higher education and a Catholic press.[7] The one major change in the picture initiated by Johan Maurits after arriving in the colony was his permitting the presence, most of the time at any rate, of the mendicant orders in New Holland, retaining only the ban on the Jesuits, though even this was not consistently adhered to, being interrupted in 1639 when a number of Carmelites, Benedictines, and Franciscans were rounded up on grounds of the threat to security, confined for a time to Fort Oranje on the off-shore island of Itamaracá, and then deported to the Caribbean.

Toleration of the Catholic faith, then, was only partial, especially with regard to denying access to the Catholic hierarchy outside Dutch Brazil. Then, in addition, one must bear in mind that there was no provision under the rules of 1629, and no formal toleration was ever instituted for the practice of the Lutheran faith, despite the large number of Lutheran soldiers and sailors in the Company's service in Brazil as in its other conquests. Nor was there any provision for tolerating Dutch Protestants who were

Frans Post, *Franciscan cloister in Brazil* (after 1660). The buildings of the regular clergy remained a feature in the landscape of Dutch Brazil.

21

Frans Post, *Boa Vista Palace* (1643). The French Church in Mauricia, constructed in 1642, is depicted in the background (F). It was the only church to be built by the Dutch in Brazil, and the *predikant* Vincente Soler delivered his sermons here. After the expulsion of the Dutch, the building was adapted by the Jesuits for Catholic worship.

neither Reformed nor Lutheran, whether Mennonites, other kinds of Anabaptists, Remonstrants or Socinians. Indeed, as in the strongholds of the Dutch East India Company in Asia, and in Dutch South Africa, until the late eighteenth century there continued to be no toleration of Lutheran, Mennonite or Remonstrant worship. Hence, if it is true that royal policy in New France had the consequence of restricting emigration from the metropolis to the colony, ultimately to its disadvantage, it is legitimate to ask whether, even if to a lesser extent, something of the sort was not true also of Dutch Brazil.

Meanwhile, the Dutch Reformed Church, with the support of the States General in The Hague, and the Heren XIX, endeavoured to organize itself in an effective manner as the public church in 'New Holland' as Dutch Brazil was officially designated. Although the first two salaried *predikanten* arrived in 1633, it was not until 1635 that clear and detailed guidelines for the organization of the Reformed faith in Dutch Brazil were laid down. It was stipulated that there should be eight or nine fully qualified *predikanten*

Joan Blaeu, Wall map of Dutch Brazil (1643, detail). The illustration shows the Dutch efforts in rural Brazil to educate and convert the local inhabitants. The church is visible in the background. The efforts of the *predikanten* enjoyed only limited success.

permanently in residence, paid for by the Company and ministering to the garrison and the civilian Protestant community, providing primary education for their children and officiating at public ceremonies. In December 1636, a Reformed consistory was set up in Recife and provision made for establishing more consistories in the future, as indeed transpired at Frederikstad, capital of the region of Paraíba, and other places. The Synod representing the Reformed consistories of all New Holland convened for the first time just a few weeks before Johan Maurits's arrival.

By 1641, according to the Spanish Calvinist *predikant*, Vincente Joachim Soler (a minister to the French Reformed Church established in Recife in the early 1640s and a preacher who also regularly delivered Calvinist sermons in his blend of Hispano-Portuguese and wrote Reformed catechisms in Spanish) there were then nineteen Reformed ministers in all in the colony and two candidates in theology assisting them in their work.[8] These clergymen ministered to a combined military, naval, and civilian Protestant population estimated by modern scholars at around 13,000, though among the French there were also, it seems, a substantial number of 'papists' who, given their circumstances, were presumably strongly discouraged from consorting with the Catholic Portuguese.

The Reformed Synod of New Holland saw it as its task not just to minister to and educate the Protestant population of the colony, guiding non-Reformed Protestant soldiers, sailors, and civilians towards a Calvinist understanding of theology, church discipline, and schooling, but also to combat drunkenness, immorality, and licentiousness, vice being considered particularly rampant among the soldiery and seamen in the town of Recife. It was also supposedly their task to convert Indians, 'indoctrinate' black slaves where possible; and, an area in which they were more active, curb, insofar as it was within their power to do so, what they considered the excessive liberty Catholics and Jews had arrogated to themselves over and beyond what was permitted under a strict reading of the Company's regulators.[9] In particular, the Reformed consistory sought to put a stop to open-air Catholic religious ceremonies and processions in the streets, oblige Catholics and others to respect Calvinist notions of the solemnity of the Lord's Day, and secure from the Governor-General an order forbidding the Jews to establish 'public' synagogues, that is large purpose-built houses of worship. Their aim was to confine Jewish ceremonies to the interiors of private residences and behind closed doors so that their cult and rituals should not offend Christian eyes.

Johan Maurits, according to Soler, though maintaining the limited freedom of practice already granted to the Jews, privately detested this group, a claim which might in fact be true. In any case, the exceptional and altogether remarkable degree of toleration enjoyed by the Jewish community in Dutch Brazil was clearly not the result of the Governor-General's personal benevolence or any intrinsic preference for, or disposition towards, toleration on the part of the WIC, but rather the consequence of sheer, straightforward necessity. During the early 1630s, most of the sugar plantations in Recife area had been destroyed in the fighting and there was no obvious way to restore the region's former flourishing and profitable condition quickly, or indeed in the medium term, other than to encourage the remaining Portuguese planters to reinvest heavily in their plantations and sugar mills and purchase fresh slaves and equipment.

However, the planters in most cases, having lately suffered ruin, and with trade at a standstill, had no cash. Moreover, such a strategy, directly financed by the WIC, would have required the Company to lay out huge sums, on credit, for purchasing supplies; which, given its already overstretched expenditures on its military and naval bases and garrisons in the Caribbean and West Africa as well as in Brazil, and its rapidly mounting

National Archives, The Hague, Arch. OWIC, nr. 52. The document lists the numbers of African slaves the Dutch West India Company transported between September 1636 and April 1637. This transport was among the first organised efforts of the WIC to enter the Atlantic slave trade. The trade in black slaves remained a monopoly of the Company.

Aernout Nagtegael, *Portrait of Isaac Aboab da Fonseca* (1685-86). Aboab arrived in Pernambuco in 1642 to become the first rabbi in the New World. He remained in Recife until the Dutch surrendered to the Portuguese in 1654.

debts – which tended to have the unwelcome effect of depressing the value of WIC shares on the Amsterdam stock exchange – was something the Company was simply in no position to contemplate. The Company lacked sufficient funds even to finance its own trading operations at a satisfactory level and felt compelled to draw in private commercial finance.[10] Consequently, there was probably no alternative to the strategy which was in fact adopted, of encouraging Portuguese Jewish emigrants from Amsterdam (and other places in western Europe, including Livorno), in most cases drawing on the capital resources of fathers, brothers, and cousins remaining in Holland, to settle in sizeable numbers in and around Recife; and allowing them to become the main brokers and intermediaries supplying the cash, credit, and supplies needed to get the region's sugar production in full flow again.[11] For only the Sephardic Jews of Holland were both Portuguese and Dutch-speaking, and combined these skills with an expert knowledge of the sugar industry, and of the Dutch market as well as resources of capital.

While the WIC retained its monopoly over the importing of black slaves shipped from West Africa, and over the export of Brazilwood, a red dyewood much utilized in the textile industry in the Low Countries and elsewhere, its straightened circumstances induced the Company to turn over to the Jews most of the business of supplying goods, slaves, and credit; and to the planters within the colony the corresponding business of buying up the raw sugar in the hinterland. While only a very few of the Jews who settled in Brazil themselves acquired plantations or sugar mills, by the late 1630s many of those based in Recife, Frederikstad, Mauricia and elsewhere where the Dutch had fortified bases regularly travelled into the interior to do business with the planters. Increasingly, and in contrast to Amsterdam and other Dutch cities where they were then permitted to reside, Jews were also allowed to own shops and engage in general retail trade. The result was the emergence of a new kind of Sephardic Jewish society, one based on a wide range of trade and finance linked to tropical agriculture and a slave economy. By 1644, when the Jewish community in Dutch Brazil reached its zenith, there were some 1,450 Jews in the colony, comprising a large proportion of its civilian non-Catholic white population.[12]

Already remarkably broad under Johan Maurits, the privileges accorded to the Jews in New Holland were further extended following the outbreak of the Portuguese planters' revolt against Dutch rule in 1645, a rebellion which led to the rapid devastation of the plantations and the ruin of the colony's only recently revived economy. Economically, the revolt by the planters, many of whom were deeply indebted to Jews, was a tremendous blow. Prodded by the elders of the Portuguese Jewish community of Amsterdam, the States General directed the Heren XIX to remove many of the remaining restrictions on Jewish retailing and entry into the professions, and ease the restrictions on the practice of their religion. This notable development was later to have important reverberations in the areas under Dutch rule in the Guyanas and the Caribbean, as well as in New Netherland, where it was by no means deemed automatic that the Jews should enjoy the same rights which they previously had the benefit of in Dutch Brazil. Although the Jews, *qua* Jews, were still excluded from all public functions and offices, and there were still some points in dispute (notably the disagreement about whether the Jews had the right to open their shops and engage in business on the Christian Sabbath, closing only on their own Sabbath) the degree of toleration accorded to this group by the late 1640s was, from any historical perspective, something wholly unprecedented in the Christian world since ancient times.[13]

At no stage, though, did the WIC regard the form of toleration established in its colony in Brazil as proscriptive for its other territories and conquests. Hence, in a letter of 26 April 1655 to the governor of New Netherland, Pieter Stuyvesant, the directors responded to complaints from the Calvinist burghers of New Amsterdam regarding the recent arrival of Sephardic refugees from Recife, following the final surrender of Dutch Brazil to the Portuguese crown, by declaring that in principle they would have liked to have granted their request that the Jews be expelled from New Netherland but, after considering the matter carefully, had concluded this would be 'unreasonable and unfair' given the Jews' heavy losses in Brazil. They pointed out that it would also be imprudent, certainly from their point of view, given the 'large amount of capital which they have invested in the shares of the Company'.[14] As a result, the Sephardim were permitted to remain and permanently settle in New Netherland but had to put up with more restricted rights, economic and religious, than they had previously enjoyed in New Holland.

28

This same tendency to claw back what had been granted to the Jews in Dutch Brazil after Johan Maurits's departure is also evident in the case of the Curaçao Islands: Curaçao, Bonaire and Aruba, as well as Tobago, or New Walcheren, an island which in the 1650s the WIC was interested in developing as a Caribbean trading depot. On these islands, not only was no provision made for Catholic or Lutheran worship, but in the first two contracts the Company directors, while allowing the Jewish colonists to settle and to engage in plantation agriculture, expressly denied the Jews permission to trade between the islands or export their horses, logwood and other resources, hoping to monopolize these activities itself.[15]

Hence the degree of freedom enjoyed by the Jews in Dutch Brazil can be seen to have been a special case, as indeed was the freedom extended to Catholics. Strategic considerations, and especially the intensifying colonial struggle with Spain and Portugal, served to widen and bolster Jewish status in Brazil in the 1630s and 1640s; and later, during the 1660s and 1670s, had a similar effect in the Dutch New World colonies, especially Curaçao and Surinam, in the context of the escalating Dutch colonial conflict with England and France. However, in contrast to Brazil, in the Guyanas and the Caribbean, no comparable strategic considerations served to bolster the position of the Catholics, Lutherans or Protestant dissenters. So far were the privileges enjoyed by the Jewish community in late seventeenth and early eighteenth-century Surinam and Curaçao from being integral to a wider programme of religious toleration and economic liberalism endorsed and sponsored by the West India Company, that there seems to have been no official willingness to allow the public practice of the Catholic and Lutheran faiths until well into the eighteenth century. On Curaçao, Bonaire and Aruba (despite the fact that most of the blacks and half-castes were Catholics and tended to play no part in the Reformed Church, receiving such religious ministering as they received from priests from nearby Venezuela who visited the island informally and sporadically, working under the auspices of the bishop of Caracas who considered the Dutch-occupied island to be part of his diocese[16]), open Catholic worship was allowed only from the 1730s and Lutheran worship not until the 1740s. In Surinam, remarkably, the ban on Catholic worship was not lifted until as late as 1787. Even in the case of the Jews, the specific toleration prevailing after 1667 in Surinam did not entail the extension of comparable Jewish

Frans Post, *Settlement in Brazil* (1654). The building in the background was presumably used as a Reformed Church when Post witnessed it, but it previously had been built and used by the Portuguese for Catholic worship.

privileges, on a lasting basis, to the West Guyana colonies of Berbice, Essequibo, and Pomeroon.

The toleration entrenched in Dutch Brazil, then, was essentially a pragmatic matter tailored to suit the harsh circumstances of an embattled colony which, in turn, raises serious questions as to whether, since it was in no way a matter of principle, the toleration established there can or should be celebrated by us today. Being unprecedented, the degree of religious toleration instituted in Dutch Brazil is of appreciable historical significance. Yet the fact remains that noone sought to justify or legitimate it in theoretical terms. As a practical exemplum, nor did it become a model for subsequent WIC practice or indeed anywhere else. Furthermore, any purely *de facto* toleration built on a system of exemptions or concessions within a basically theological framework, such as that which arose in New Holland, seems inevitably to be prone, precisely because it is perceived as lacking in legitimacy, to place a particular emphasis on symbolic points, such as the closure of Jewish shops on Sundays – an issue argued over in Surinam until deep into the eighteenth century – leading to restrictive rulings which, however marginal in the wider toleration context, keep alive a sense of the propriety and fittingness of institutionalized curbs on individual freedom of thought, belief, and expression.

1   See, in particular, José Antonio Gonsalves de Mello, 'Vincent Joachim Soler in Dutch Brazil', in: Van den Boogaart, ed., *Johan Maurits van Nassau-Siegen* (1604-1679) (The Hague 1979) 249.
2   Mário Neme, *Fórmulas Políticas no Brasil Holandês* (São Paulo 1971) 158-60.
3   British Library, London, MS. Egerton 1131 fols. 295v-96, 306, *Consulta of the Consejo de Estado*, Madrid, 24 Sept. 1624; C. R. Boxer, *The Dutch in Brazil 1624-1654* (Oxford 1957) 14-15; Jonathan Israel, *Diasporas Within a Diaspora: Jews, Crypto-Jews and the World Maritime Empires (1540-1740)* (Boston, Cologne, and Leiden 2002) 146-47.
4   C. R. Boxer, *Salvador de Sá and the Struggle for Brazil and Angola*, 1602-1686 (London 1952) 44-56.
5   Boxer, *The Dutch in Brazil*, 3-16; Jonathan Israel, 'El Brasil y la política holandesa en el Nuevo Mundo (1618-1648)' in: *Acuarela de Brasil 500 Años Despues* (Salamanca 2000) 17-19.
6   Neme, *Fórmulas Políticas no Brasil*, 158.
7   Ibid., 166-69.
8   Gonsalves de Mello, 'Vincent Joachim Soler in Dutch Brazil', 249.
9   Neme, *Fórmulas Políticas no Brasil*, 170-71.
10 P. J. van Winter, *De Westindische Compagnie ter kamer Stad en Lande* (The Hague 1978) 135-42, 154-55.
11 Boxer, *The Dutch in Brazil*, 133-44; Arnold Wiznitzer, *Jews of Colonial Brazil* (Morningside Heights, NY 1960) 120-38; Jonathan Israel, 'The Jews of Dutch America', in: P. Bernardini and Norman Fiering, eds., *The Jews and the Expansion of Europe to the West, 1450-1800* (New York 2001) 340-42.
12 Arnold Wiznitzer, 'The number of Jews in Dutch Brazil (1630-1654)' *Jewish Social Studies* XVI (1954) 107-14; Wiznitzer, *Jews of Colonial Brazil*, 120-38; I. S. Emmanuel, 'Seventeenth-century Brazilian Jewry: a critical review' *American Jewish Archives* XIV (1962) 32-68.
13 Ibid.; Israel, *Diasporas*, 367-72.
14 Quoted in G. L. Smith, *Religion and Trade in New Netherland: Dutch Origins and American Development* (Cornell, Ithaca 1973) 214.
15 G. H. Cone, 'The Jews of Curaçao according to documents from the Archives of the State of New York', *Publications of the American Jewish Historical Society* X (1902) 143, 147-49; I. S. and S. A. Emmanuel, *History of the Jews of the Netherlands Antilles* (2 vols; Cincinatti 1970) I, 43; Israel, 'Jews of Dutch America', 345; for New Walcheren, see Mordechai Arbell, 'The failure of the Jewish settlement on the Island of Tobago', *Proceedings of the Eleventh World Congress of Jewish Studies* (1994) vol. I ii, 304-05.
16 Carlos Felice Cardot, *Curazao Hispánico: Antagonismo Flamenco-Español* (Caracas 1973) 392-410; Wim Klooster, 'Between Habsburg neglect and Bourbon assertiveness: Hispano-Dutch relations in the New World, 1650-1750', in: A. Crespo Solana and Manuel Herrero Sánchez, eds., *España y las 17 Provincias de los Países Bajos* (Córdoba 2002) 714-15.

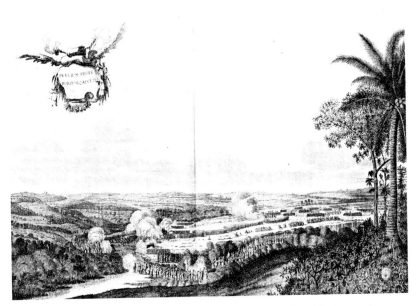

Frans Post, *Battle at Porto Calvo (1637)* (1645, detail) between Dutch and Portuguese troops, published in Barlaeus's *Rerum per octennium in Brasilia* (Amsterdam 1647).

Stuart B. Schwartz

Portuguese Attitudes of Religious Tolerance in Dutch Brazil

In the history of toleration, the occupation of north-eastern Brazil by the Dutch West India Company, and especially the period of the government of Count Johan Maurits of Nassau-Siegen (1637-44), is sometimes presented as a kind of Camelot on the Capiberibe, a moment when under the protection of a humanist governor and an enlightened Renaissance prince, Catholics, Protestants, and Jews were able to live in relative peace and tranquility, a peace and harmony that in its concessions to freedom of conscience and of worship exceeded even that of Amsterdam itself.[1]

Toleration, or the multi-confessional state, we should remember was viewed by most governments at the time as a prescription for internal dissent and disloyalty. We now know that Johan Maurits did not have an easy time in enforcing such a policy. He had to struggle continually against the intransigence of most of the *predikanten* of the local Calvinist ministry as well as the demands by the directors of the West India Company for a less tolerant policy in the colony. Moreover, he faced steadfast opposition to his government and the presence of the Dutch from many of the resident Catholic clergy, directed in their opposition by the bishop of Salvador, the capital of Portuguese Brazil.[2]

This doctrinal opposition to Johan Maurits's pragmatism in matters of religion was accompanied by the use of rhetoric of conflict that increasingly became a reality after Johan Maurits was recalled by the West India Company and an uprising of the Portuguese residents (The War of Divine Liberation, 1645-54) broke out. The ties of political interest and religious affiliation, long present but now stimulated by wartime rhetoric and propaganda after 1645, hardened along national and religious lines, and the bellicose discourse of both sides emphasized the heretical nature of their opponents, disguising to some extent a period of political and social collaboration or at least the relativism and indifference that had preceded it.

Most studies of Dutch Brazil have explained the ideological and practical reasons for a policy of toleration as an extension of Dutch practice and interests without much explanation of why and how the Luso-Brazilian residents, the *moradores* as well as the free Indian population, participated and cooperated, at least for a while, in this experiment in tolerance. It seems to me possible to examine the forces among the inhabitants on the other side that led, at least for a while, to a period of collaboration and even conviviality between the Dutch and the Portuguese. In short, was there a possibility of a more open or tolerant Portuguese society (one without an Inquisition) that was revealed in the brief period of the Dutch occupation of north-eastern Brazil, especially during the government of Johan Maurits of Nassau?

The first problem in answering such a question is the historiography of toleration itself. Most of it has woven together two historically separate strands into a single story. First, this history has remained, for the most part, almost exclusively in the hands of intellectual historians; and the story that they have chosen to tell is that of a chain of theologians, philosophers, and statesmen who from the early Middle Ages began to raise the issues of freedom of conscience and belief that ultimately resulted in the policies of toleration codified in the eighteenth century, and eventually became state policy in much of Europe in the nineteenth century. The list of names varies from author to author or from collected volume to collected volume, and the sub-themes of rationalism, scepticism, atheism, and *raison d'etat* have also developed as essential elements of the story; but the litany of figures is relatively well-known and has usually at least included Erasmus, Spinoza, Locke, and Voltaire.[3] Second, this intellectual history has often been set in a context of political realities that traced the horrors of the wars of religion and the persecution of dissenters in the sixteenth century during the Protestant and Catholic Reformations; and emphasized how, by the mid-seventeenth century, a Europe exhausted by war and fratricidal bloodletting witnessed the emergence of religious tolerance based often as much on practical considerations as on moral or intellectual conviction.[4] While early arrangements of toleration usually made definite distinctions between public and private religious practice and placed limitations on the former, some kind of religious toleration had emerged by the seventeenth century because the bloody cost of intolerance had simply risen too high.[5]

Theodore de Bry, *America* VI (1596) ill. xvii. The engraving shows the cruel practices of the conquistadors in the New World, in this case in Florida. Illustrations with this theme circulated in Northern Europe, enhancing the notion of Spanish intolerance.

By the second half of that century there was a growing number of states and rulers – Colbert in France, Cromwell in England, Frederick II in Prussia – who for practical considerations had moved toward a position of sufferance or toleration of religious diversity and dissent. The advantages of such policies were not hidden from view. The tremendous economic growth of Amsterdam was felt by many observers to be a paradigmatic case, the result of its toleration and its practical approach to religion.[6] Similar interpretations were sometimes extended to explain the rise of England, France, and Prussia.[7]

In the telling of these interrelated histories of toleration, Spain, Portugal, and their American colonies have had virtually no place whatever. The Iberian kingdoms had experienced a long period during the Middle

Ages when Christians, Jews, and Muslims had all lived together in a close but often tense and violent relationship. As the Christian kingdoms expanded, the followers of other religions were first reduced in status, and then subjected to conversions or expulsions. The elimination of Jews and Muslims from the Christian kingdoms, the suppression of emerging Protestant cells, and the establishment of Inquisition tribunals to ensure orthodoxy, all ensured the unity of the Iberian monarchies as Catholic kingdoms that became, with few exceptions, entrenched in most histories as classic examples of intolerance whose stories provided exemplary and cautionary examples of how fanaticism, dogmatism, intolerance and the Inquisition could so oppress a people as to close them off from all enlightenment and progress. What better way to explain 'the backwardness' of the Spaniards and Portuguese and the progressivism of the French, English or Germanic peoples than to look at the closing of the Hispanic mind due to intolerance. Iberia was clearly a zone of intolerance, and despite an occasional thinker like Bartholomé de Las Casas or Francisco de Vitoria, or the unsuccessful attempts at a Colbertian kind of tolerance toward the Jews by the Count-Duke of Olivares in Spain or by the Jesuit Father António Vieira in Portugal, most scholars considered Spain and Portugal unfertile ground for the history of toleration.

These countries, for example, played no role at all in the great work of the French Jesuit, Joseph Lecler, whose *Toleration and the Reformation* (1955) was the standard history of its day that told in detail the story of the subtle variations in the positions of individual thinkers against the background of the changing politics of a Europe torn by religious strife. For Lecler, and for many of the historians of early modern religion, the story to tell was the disintegration of Christian unity and the rise of confessionalization. But Lecler, while writing an essentially intellectual history of great thinkers, recognized that the humanists, churchmen, politicians, and ordinary citizens of his story all belonged to a 'particular social milieu' and that 'this whole social milieu was already aware of the same issues'. In other words, Lecler recognized that the history of toleration was not simply an exercise in elite intellectual history, it involved society as a whole, what he called 'milieu', and while he had neither the inclination nor the methodology to recover that history, he recognized that the relationship between society and the 'heroes of tolerance' was a vital but unknown part of the story.

It is exactly that milieu and its relationship to the idea of religious tolerance or pluralism that fascinates me. I have been carrying out a study of attitudes of tolerance in Spain, Portugal, and their American colonies, not in terms of government and Church policy which were by intention and conviction intolerant, but in terms of attitudes held by people from various social strata, lay and clerical. I have found considerable evidence of ideas of religious relativism and tolerance that came from a variety of sources. Despite the fact that the Catholic Church's position by the end of the fifteenth century was *nulla salus extra ecclesia* (no salvation outside the Church), there was an older theological tradition of Pelagian thought and a tradition of natural law that had left theologically open the possibility of salvation for those who followed other faiths, or were ignorant of the Church's message. Moreover, among the many common 'propositions' of a heterodox, deviant, or heretical nature that included doubts about the existence of heaven, hell or purgatory, the efficacy of the saints, the virginity of Mary, the authority of the Pope, the presence of Christ in the Eucharist, or the sinfulness of sex outside of marriage, there existed an ancient belief that was commonly repeated, that *'cada um pode-se salvar na sua ley'* ('each person can be saved in their own law').

This idea was repeated on many occasions, often by very common people, and while it was sometimes expressed by the descendants of converted Jews (New Christians) or of converted Muslims (*moriscos*) who we might expect to hold this idea as a way of defending their former faith and thus affirming the salvation of their ancestors, it was an idea that was also sometimes expressed by clerics who looked back to the earlier medieval debates and more frequently by the Old Christian lay population. During an Inquisitorial visit to the Portuguese Alentejo from 1578 to 1579, for example, Manuel Rodrigues, an Old Christian, raised questions about the justice of Portugal's campaigns in North Africa. He warned that 'only God knew if this war was just or unjust because the Muslims were also his creatures', and when told that all the Muslims were condemned to hell, he answered that 'only God knew if they went there or not'. In that same inquest, a certain Lianor Martins complained that Dom Sebastião's campaigns in Morocco had unmade many marriages and caused many people to be lost because he had not allowed each person to live in his or her law: the Jews in theirs, the Muslims in theirs, and the Old Christians in theirs.[8]

This sentiment was voiced repeatedly across the Iberian world and while we have more examples of it in Spain than in Portugal, that situation is probably more evidence of the primary interest of the Inquisition in Portugal in crypto-Judaism rather than a lack of this proposition in the minds or hearts of the population.

The roots of this idea were varied. To some extent they seem to have been a common sense understanding of the diversity of beliefs in the world and a recognition that good could be found in many peoples and faiths. Sometimes it was an idea voiced by doubters and sceptics, but more often by people who thought of themselves as good Catholics who simply could not understand why a merciful or omnipotent God would condemn so many people who had lived before the coming of Christ, or who had lived a good life according to natural law, even if they were outside the Church. Sometimes there was a kind of Rabelaisian practicality in their statements.[9] Such thinking also led people to oppose the use of force in matters of conscience. Julian de Anguieta, a resident in Cuenca, Spain told Inquisitors in 1662 that it was wrong to take from each person his free will to believe what he wants and to oblige Christians to believe by force the law of Jesus Christ, and it seemed to him wrong and against the teachings of Christian doctrine.[10] Inocencio de Aldama, an Old Christian from Alava in the Basque country who had soldiered in Italy and lived a vagabond life, told Inquisitors in Murcia that he would believe whatever they told him was correct, but that not even the 'doctors of Salamanca' could dissuade him that 'each person has his own path', and 'that all the religions came from the same stock from which different roots appear, and all of them bear fruit, and each person could be saved in the law they chose, so long as they followed it responsibly'.[11]

But while these practical, rationalistic defenses were often voiced, this was, on the other hand, an important theological issue over which the early Church Fathers had struggled greatly. It brought into question central issues of Christian doctrine, the relative value of grace and good works and the validity of free will (*libre albedrio*). While the Church and Inquisition had adopted a strict Augustinian position by the fifteenth century, the controversy did not abate, and it extended into the seventeenth century in Spain where the Jesuits accused the Dominicans of a kind of Lutheranism for placing too much emphasis on grace, while the Dominicans retaliated by accusing the Jesuits of being quasi-Pelagians for overemphasizing works. But while theologians recognized the important issues at stake in these debates, they were also aware of the potential dangers that these difficult questions raised. In 1689, when a number of Portuguese theologians were asked to comment on the possibility that a Calvinist or Lutheran, baptized in his own faith, might be saved, one wrote that 'the response should not be given in front of less prudent people [because] that might result in some scandal or spiritual harm'.[12]

By the sixteenth century, despite a concerted effort by the post-Tridentine Church to suppress any deviance in this regard, such ideas could still be found among occasional clerics (usually Franciscans) and among many common people, workers, sailors, soldiers, shopkeepers, New Christians and Old Christians, and sometimes among foreigners; Italians, French, Flemish, and others. Juan Falcó from Narbonne expressed the universalist belief of many that 'Christians, Huguenots, Lutherans, and Jews all believed in only one God'. When told that only those who were baptized and believed in the Holy Mother Church could be saved, he answered with an argument based both on tolerance and common sense: 'Neither you nor I can say that [...] and if everyone is going to hell the devils will have too much to do'. As for the Jews, he recalled Christ's words: 'Father forgive them for they know not what they do'.

Many of these people had travelled; often they could read and write, but did not have university educations. Some accused of this proposition had been prisoners in North Africa, and despite their captivity had developed an appreciation for Islamic culture. Others had lived, worked or soldiered in Europe where they had come into contact with Protestants.[13] Others of those accused demonstrated a considerable curiosity about different religions, some an indifference to all religions, and some, among them priests and friars, even a kind of religious malleability that made their identification with any one faith insecure. Many, however, held that only God knew which of the laws or religions was true, and that force in matters of conscience such as the forced conversion of Jews or wars of religion against Protestants was an error. After attending an *auto de fe* in Valladolid where Lutherans were burned, Francisco de Amores told his wife that the intolerant sermon preached there was against the teachings of Christ. He argued: 'Each can save himself in his own law, the Moor in his, the Jew in his, the Christian in his and the Lutheran in his'.[14]

These ideas circulated widely. They were certainly current in the Sephardic community in Amsterdam. A case in point is that of Juan (Daniel) Prado and Isaac Orobio de Castro, two Sephardic converts who had originally met in 1635 when both were studying theology at the University of Alcalá. They had become good friends long before either had left Spain or professed Judaism. Later, under examination by the Inquisition, Orobio had reported that Prado had told him on that earlier occasion that 'all men are entitled to redemption, each in virtue of his own religion – Jews, Muslim and Christian are entitled to eternal happiness, because all three religions have political aims, the source of which lies in natural law, which in Aristotle's philosophy is styled the *causa causarum'*.

Later Prado also told Orobio that all religions have the capacity to bring their followers to salvation. Prado at that time was apparently still a loyal member of the Church. Later in Holland, the two friends were to become bitter intellectual rivals, Prado representing a skepticism about Judaism's exclusive validity and Orobio a defender of that religion's messianic role. Some have argued that Prado's universalism shared roots with Spinoza's scepticism and that all of these ideas were an outgrowth of the *converso* experience and situation. But such ideas were also circulating widely among the Old Christian population of Spain as well, and even though Prado had mentioned the philosophical basis of such ideas, he had done so in the traditional popular formula, that 'each can be saved in his own law'.[15]

While such attitudes could be found throughout the Iberian world, we know more about them in Spain and its colonies than in Portugal and its dominions. The Portuguese Inquisition was primarily oriented toward the prosecution of New Christians as crypto-Jews and around eighty percent of all its prosecutions were for that crime. Thus other offenses like these heretical propositions received far less attention and left far less evidence than those in the Spanish tribunals.

The Portuguese Inquisition conducted a consistent campaign to extirpate Judaism and to denigrate the New Christians among the general population, but not everyone agreed. Of course, there was the famous case of the Jesuit, Padre António Vieira, who opposed the persecution of the Jews for primarily mercantilist reasons and who actually had the Inquisition suspended for a short period (1674-81) but Vieira was not alone.[16]

In 1623, André Lopes, known as 'The Harp', an Old Christian wool merchant but married to a New Christian, was arrested by the Inquisition

Late nineteenth-century portrait of Padre António Vieira,
based on seventeenth-century illustrations.

of Evora for criticizing the Inquisition's policies. He claimed the people
punished in *autos de fe* were martyrs for their faith, and he had refused to
attend an *auto de fe* in that city. He told friends that just as there had been
lightning bolts from heaven when St. Barbara was martyred, he refused to

attend these public ceremonies because these people were also martyrs. The Inquisition's actions he said, were only performed 'to eat and spend the property of those arrested'. And when the town fool had remarked about the erection of a platform or *cadafalso* for an *auto de fe* and had quipped *'cadafalso e bem falso'* ('a stage of punishment and really false'), Lopes had said 'sometimes the mad speak truths'. One accuser felt that Lopes was more a Jew than his wife, but another friend, the Old Christian tailor Domingos Gomes, remembered Lopes's hypothetical question: if God did not want the New Christians to be Christians, why did the Inquisitorial gentlemen wish to make them Christians by force?[17]

At about the same time, another case scandalized the Lisbon Inquisition. An inquisitorial visit to Brazil in 1618 had produced a large number of prisoners, many of them New Christians, who had been sent to Lisbon for their trials. On 25 September 1620, the jailer of the Inquisitorial prison reported that during the night shots had been fired in the city and that these had actually been signals for the prisoners that a general pardon had been signed in Madrid and that one of the Inquisitors had suddenly died. In other words, these were communications designed to give heart to the prisoners and to strengthen their resolve not to confess. But what the bailiff had told the Inquisitors was even more troublesome.

The man who was interpreting these signals and who was organizing the resistance of the New Christian prisoners to the tribunal was a Catholic priest, Father Fernando Pereira de Castro, who had already earned a reputation in the prison for speaking out loudly in favor of New Christians, arguing that they were unjustly imprisoned and that the Inquisitors had exceeded their authority. If the New Christians remained firm, he promised, all would be released with 'great honour'.

One might have expected that Pereira de Castro was himself a New Christian, but that was not the case. He had been born in Goa and he was by his appearance and speech identified as a *mestiço*, that is, the child of a Portuguese and an Indian woman. Son of a *fidalgo*, he had grown up in the Estado da India, and like many of the young men of the Portuguese colony, he had become a soldier; but he also had a taste for reading and he eventually entered the priesthood, a somewhat exceptional situation since *mestiço* priests, although not unknown, were relatively rare. Pereira de Castro eventually travelled to Lisbon, studied at Coimbra, and then travelled to Brazil and Spain as well as visiting Milan and Rome.

He returned to Brazil in the retinue of a governor but there got into trouble and was arrested by the ecclesiastical administrator in Rio de Janeiro, supposedly for sexual contact with young men.[18] He denied the charge and even under torture he continued to claim instead that he had been imprisoned 'because he knew of the tyrannies done here to the New Christians and prisoners, and that he had been arrested not for being a Jew or a sodomite, but because he knew the truth about the business of the New Christians'.[19] Eventually, he was suspended from the priesthood and sent to six years of penal exile at the furthest corner of the Portuguese empire, the Ilha do Príncipe, a rock in the south Atlantic.

Whether Pereira de Castro was a homosexual or not is impossible to know, but he had taken on the cause of the New Christians and he was sure that this stance was the cause of his troubles. Soldier and priest, like many of the *tolerantes* in the Iberian world, he had lived in other lands and knew other cultures. Perhaps better educated than many of his contemporaries, his attitudes toward the New Christians had come at an importune moment in the midst of the struggle over the pardons. But he perceived the situation of the New Christians as unjust and had not only been willing to speak against it, but also to stimulate or organize resistance to the Inquisition even in the prison.

These cases indicate the existence of an attitude of resistance toward the official position of the Church in matters of the definition of heresy and a willingness to accommodate religious difference, or at least to concede to individuals the benefit of the doubt in matters of conscience. Brazil was a particular case in that regard since New Christians had composed a large percentage of the original settlers and had become integrated into all aspects of the colony's life. Integrated so well, in fact, that at times when official policy was persecution by Inquisitorial investigation, many people refused to testify or offer usable evidence.[20]

Of course, such ideas of resistance to the exclusive claims of the Church were not limited to the Iberian peninsula or to any one social group. Anyone familiar with Boccaccio's tale of the three rings, or with the discourse of the miller Menocchio in Carlo Ginzburg's *The Cheese and the Worms*, or with the scepticism of the *Traité des Trois Imposteurs* will recognize that currents of thought that challenged the exclusive validity of any one religion (or of any at all) had long existed in Europe, and despite the policies of crown and Church, even in Spain, Portugal, and their overseas colonies.

Portuguese Responses to
Religious Toleration in Dutch Brazil

Even before the arrival of Johan Maurits in 1637, the West India Company
(WIC) had sought to neutralize Portuguese resistance by promising the
Luso-Brazilian inhabitants, the *moradores*, the security of their property and
positive economic benefits as well as freedom of conscience and belief.
This was made clear in the general outline for rule of the colony set out in
1629. The WIC had been founded to carry out a war against the king of
Spain and his possessions, and although Spain and Portugal were under the
same monarch, the WIC had targeted Brazil to some extent because it hoped
that the inhabitants might be less inclined to resist given the traditional
enmity between Portuguese and Castilians. Of course, Portugal was a
Catholic kingdom, but Holland had been a major trading partner with
Portugal since the Middle Ages and, in fact, had carried much of the
early Brazilian sugar trade. Religious differences were not seen as an insur-
mountable obstacle to renewed collaboration. Moreover, there were various
groups in the Brazilian colony who might find advantage or benefit in
cooperation with the Dutch. After the Dutch occupation of Salvador from
1624 to 1625, a large number of inhabitants of the Portuguese colony had
been tried for collaboration. These included black slaves and freemen,
New Christians, and a surprising number of Old Christians as well.

After the Dutch returned in 1630 and seized Pernambuco, they immediately
found that some kind of religious toleration had to be extended if the colony
and its sugar economy was to function at all. Sometimes the pressures came
from surprising directions. The Dutch and other foreigners who acquired
Brazilian sugar mills quickly learned that the slaves simply refused to work
if, at the beginning of the harvest (*safra*), the mill and the workers were
not blessed, sprinkled with holy water, and an appropriate prayer said
by a priest. Despite complaints by members of the Reformed Church about
such 'idolatry', the practice was generally allowed. Portuguese sugar
planters were of course encouraged to stay by the Dutch and urged to
abandon their estates by the Portuguese because both sides knew that
without sugar the colony would fail. Johan Maurits realized that the old
Portuguese planter class was a powerful and potentially dangerous element

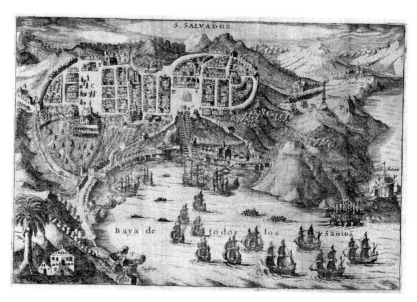

Engraving in *Reysboeck van het rijcke Brasilien* (1624), showing the Dutch conquest of San Salvador de Bahía. While they initially succeeded, they were defeated only several months later by an auxiliary fleet from Portugal.

and he hoped that eventually they might be supplanted; but he also realized that without the Portuguese cane farmers and sugar technicians, the colony could not succeed, and he sought to keep them in place.[21]

On the other hand, despite a tradition that insisted that the Dutch had little skill or interest in sugar-making, it is interesting to examine a report of the sugar mills in Dutch Brazil made in 1639. A number of the mills had been acquired by Dutch merchants or employees of the WIC, and while some of them were absentee owners, there were others like the physician Servaes Carpentier who became a resident *senhor de engenho* and remained so for the rest of his life. The 1639 report also revealed that many of the mills depended on sugar cane grown by dependent cane farmers as was the Brazilian custom, but that the Dutch and other foreigners, including merchants and men in the administration of the colony, often supplied cane alongside Portuguese cane farmers. Take, for example, Engenho Matapagipe where two Portuguese and two Dutch cane growers were contracted, or the famous Engenho Velho that had been taken by the German-born Dutch commander Sigismund von Schoppe and had one Dutch and seven

47

Theodore de Bry, *America* V (1595) ill ii. The engraving shows the various stages of the labour-intensive process of sugar production. Slaves cut and prepare the cane, and take it to the sugar mill where the liquid is extracted. The liquid is then poured into vases that are placed in the sun to dry. The illustration depicts the sixteenth-century practice before the Portuguese innovations that changed the Brazilian sugar industry in the 1610s and 1620s.

Frans Post, *Drawing of a sugar mill* (ca. 1640?). The pen drawing clearly shows the new sugar mills which became common features of Portuguese plantations in Brazil several years before the Dutch West India Company arrived.

Frans Post, *Engenho real* (ca. 1645?). The painter here depicts one of the largest *engenhos* in Dutch Brazil, the Engenho Real. The church in the background demonstrates the omnipresence of the Portuguese religious infrastructure in Brazil at the time of Dutch rule.

Portuguese cane suppliers.[22] Whether the mill owners were Portuguese or Dutch, a mixed group of cane suppliers could be found on many of the sugar estates. We know little of their relations with each other, but they certainly shared the same interests and must have seen and interacted with each other on a regular basis. Sugar created its own logic of identity and interest between the Dutch and the Portuguese.

We get some inkling of what that contact and possible collaboration and perhaps tolerance might have looked like from a Portuguese episcopal investigation that was carried out from 1635 to 1637 by Dom Pedro da Silva, Bishop of Salvador. Rumours of a certain degree of collaboration with the Dutch by members of the Catholic clergy in Paraíba had moved the bishop to conduct this inquiry, and as a result some eighty individuals were denounced: eight of them clergymen, twenty-four New Christians, and forty-eight Old Christians. The New Christians, of course, were no surprise and some of them took the opportunity offered by the Dutch invasion and the extension of religious liberty to the Jews to openly return to the Judaism of their ancestors and join their coreligionists from Europe who came to the colony. What was more surprising were the Portuguese Old Christians, both lay and clerical, who for personal or religious reasons were willing either to accept Dutch rule, were indifferent in matters of religion, or who converted to the reformed religion of the Protestants.[23]

Some of the cases were scandalous like that of the priest Frei Manoel Calado, known as Fr. Manoel 'dos Oculos' who dined and drank with the Dutch, urged his flock to accommodate their rule, invited Calvinist ministers to his home, and who became a confidant of Johan Maurits. He was a man who changed sides with ease and skill, and his later account from a pro-Portuguese perspective is still an invaluable source.[24] There was also the case of the infamous former Jesuit missionary, Manuel de Moraes, who fully went over to the Dutch, using his linguistic skills in Tupi to turn the indigenous peoples under his care to the Dutch side.[25] Many local Portuguese claimed he had provided the invaders considerable help with a sword in his hand, giving up the cloth and later marrying in Holland. The investigation also revealed that an Augustinian in Serinhaem, Frei Antonio Caldeira, had contacted the enemy, sold them crates of sugar and had dined and drank with them; a charge similar to that made against other clerics, some of whom like Frei António were reported to have urged their parishioners to remain by saying that the Dutch did no harm to anyone and that they were good people (boa gente). Father João Gomes de Aguiar was denounced for having gone to Porto Calvo and publicly eaten and toasted with the Hollanders. In public and in private he had said the Hollanders were honest men who kept their word. He had even said: 'I wish we kept our obligations to our Catholic faith as well as they kept theirs'. This was a phrase indicating a certain relativism in regard to religious belief and an admiration for the consistency of the enemy's faith.[26]

The kind of interchange on a daily basis that emerges from the denunciations reveals many reasons for collaboration or a willingness to get along. When Antonio de Caldeira da Mata, an ensign from Madeira, was asked if he knew any Catholic who had done or said anything wrong, he answered that many had done and said bad things, and he singled out Pero Lopes de Veras, a senhor do engenho who had given his allegiance to the Dutch and aided them. While there was some question if Lopes de Veras, who was married to a sister of the Portuguese commander, Matias de Albuquerque, was a New Christian, the evidence was not clear. In another instance, Matias Fidalgo remained at Cabo de Santo Agostinho after it fell to the Dutch for personal reasons since the former Portuguese governor had arrested him for cohabiting with a married woman. He was accused of befriending the invaders.

Such friendships were not impossible and sometimes mutually beneficial. The most famous of all was that of João Fernandes Vieira, the later hero of the Portuguese restoration of Brazil. Vieira, a man of humble origins from Madeira, had arrived in Brazil with few prospects. He had originally resisted the Dutch invasion, but he provided self-interested help to the High Councillor, Jacob Stachouwer, who then used Vieira as his agent and clerk. Together, based on their 'tight friendship', they made a fortune. Vieira eventually owned fifteen sugar mills and by 1637 was joining with other Portuguese, both New and Old Christians, to complain to the WIC that any plan for a monopoly of trade would be a violation of the promises they had received of 'greater liberties not only in justice and religion, but also in the development of our business and capital'. Vieira became a confidant of Johan Maurits and one of the colony's wealthiest men. His collaboration and success earned him the enmity and jealousy of many, but eventually his decision to side with the rebellion seems to have been made when the WIC began to demand that the Portuguese planters pay their loans to the Company. Vieira held the largest debt and he had good financial reasons to resist payment even though he eventually couched his resistance in terms of loyalty to Portugal and detestation of heresy.[27]

Perhaps most revealing of the possibilities of crossing confessional lines were cases like that of Martim Lopes on Itamaracá island who communicated regularly with the Dutch, acquired an Old Testament in Spanish from them (the reading of which in the vernacular was prohibited) and who had married one of his daughters to a Hollander. Despite all of the efforts of the Catholic clergy, there were many such unions. In another case, Domingos Ribeiro had married three of his daughters to Dutchmen apparently in Protestant marriages, and when someone questioned him about it, he was reported to have said that the Dutch were better Christians than the Portuguese. In another instance in Igarassú, two girls called the 'Pimentinhas', the nieces of a man called Pimenta, had married Dutchmen, their elders defending the match by saying that 'a Fleming is worth more than many

Portuguese', a paraphrase of the Old Iberian saying, 'better a good Jew than a bad Christian'.

That such unions were frequent was true not only in Pernambuco, but elsewhere in Dutch Brazil. In Rio Grande do Norte, many Dutchmen married Portuguese widows, and Padre António Vieira reported from Maranhão in 1642 that not only were there marriages, but that Portuguese men and women were accepting 'the customs and even the rituals of the Dutch'.[28] Some of the Dutch like Gaspar van der Ley who married Portuguese women became Catholics while others like Jan Wijnants of Haarlem, a *senhor de engenho* who married a planter's daughter from Goiana remained a Calvinist. One of the daughters of Mateus da Costa of Ipojuca married a New Christian who became a Jew while another married a Dutch Protestant.[29] The number of these unions was enough to cause the concern of both the Protestant and the Catholic clergy, for such marriages always implied a certain insecurity of national and religious identities. After the outbreak of hostilities in 1645, a number of locally-married Dutchmen joined the rebel cause and some enlisted in the eight companies of former employees of the WIC (most of them French and other Catholics) who joined the Luso-Brazilian forces.

Marriages between Portuguese women and Dutch soldiers; New Christians consorting with openly-practicing Jews in Recife; the circulation of prohibited books; friendships; business contacts; attendance at Calvinist Churches. All of these actions were denounced and reported in the Portuguese episcopal investigation of behaviour in occupied Brazil prior to the arrival of Johan Maurits, but with his arrival in 1637, despite his own personal reservations about Catholics and Jews, the policy of toleration was vigorously enforced and the opportunities for contact increased.[30] There continued to be tensions and sometimes scuffles over the use of churches, religious processions, and the other moments of public contact between Catholics, Protestants, and Jews. Suggestions were made by the local governing council to limit Jewish immigration and to force them to wear distinguishing badges. Despite considerable opposition, however, Johan Maurits extended the guarantes of freedom of conscience to all, and sought to incorporate local Portuguese, even clerics, into his confidence.[31]

An excellent opportunity to do so came after the Portuguese restoration of 1640 made Holland and Portugal allies against Philip IV of Spain. To celebrate the new situation, in April 1641 Johan Maurits organized a

Frans Post, *Naval battle*, published in Barlaeus's *Rerum per octennium in Brasilia* (Amsterdam 1647). The engraving depicts a naval battle before the coast of Brazil between Dutch vessels and an Iberian fleet in 1640. The *Armada* constituted the last combined Luso-Spanish attempt to defeat the Dutch in Brazil before the Portuguese regained independence from Spain. Their attempt to defeat the Dutch was unsuccessful.

Frans Post, Engraving of Dutch ships before the city of Sao Paolo in Luanda on the African coast, published in Barlaeus's *Rerum per octennium in Brasilia* (Amsterdam 1647). The Dutch muscled their way into the slave trade in Luanda in 1641 at the expense of the Portuguese, but could only maintain their favourable position until 1648.

great spectacle in Recife with horse races and equestrian competitions in which Portuguese and Dutch gentlemen paraded together and competed for the cheers and favors of the ladies as well as for various prizes. There were theatrical performances, dinners, toasts, and drinking bouts to mark the new political alliance.[32] While rivalry and competition between Portuguese and Dutch or Catholic and Protestant participants in these events lay just below the surface, politics overcame, at least momentarily, old animosities.

The era of goodwill did not last long. Dutch refusal to abandon the Brazilian colony, the Dutch attack on Luanda in 1641, the withdrawal of Johan Maurits and new demands on the West India Company's debtors, all contributed to increasing hostility between the Portuguese and the Dutch which grew from primarily political and economic considerations. Johan Maurits, however, remained an example of what was possible to achieve by toleration, and because of that, he was a danger. A multi-confessional society was a threat. Doña Margarida, the Vicereine of Portugal, warned in 1639 that the faith of the settlers and converted Indians of Brazil was imperilled by

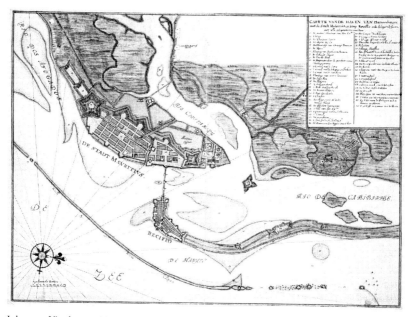

Johannes Vingboons, Map of Recife and Mauricia (ca. 1665). This map shows the capital of Dutch Brazil at the time when it was finally surrendered to the Portuguese in 1654.

contact with the Dutch enemy, and that 'carried by private interests and relations they might leave (God forbid) the Holy Faith and separate from the purity of the Christian religion'.[33]

In fact, even after 1641, while relations improved, the number of conversions was small; but Portuguese appreciation for Johan Maurits' religious and commercial policies was great. *Moradores*, Indians and blacks all cried at his departure. Portuguese settlers still referred to him as 'our Saint Anthony' and years later, in 1647, after Johan Maurits had gone back to Europe, the very possibility of his returning to Brazil was enough to make Portuguese policy-makers afraid that he might undercut the rebellion by attracting the inhabitants of Brazil to his side once again.[34] The joint inducements of liberty of trade and liberty of conscience posed a real threat.

Once the War of Divine Liberation had begun, the rhetoric of confessional animosity and national loyalties set the parameters of behavior again and were later adopted in a nationalist historiography.[35] Under ecclesiastical urgings from pulpits and on the battlefield, Luso-Brazilian forces and leaders meted out particularly harsh punishments to Catholic converts, black or

Native American allies of the Dutch, and especially to New Christians who were looked upon as heretics and turncoats. The terminology of heresy became the mould into which the war was poured, and so it becomes virtually impossible to separate the strands of economic, political, and religious motivation and justification in the struggle.

But the use of the language and concepts of religious intolerance was not uncontested. When Recife fell on 28 January 1654, the Portuguese commander Francisco Barreto treated the defeated Dutch with all the courtesies of war, abiding by the surrender agreement and enforcing strict control of his troops to prevent abuses. Even more impressive was his treatment of the remaining Jewish community despite the objections of the Inquisition, allowing them to depart unharmed, to sell their property, and even helping to provide adequate shipping for their voyage. Surely, said the Jewish chronicler Saul Levy Mortara, God had saved his people by influencing the 'heart of governor Barreto'.[36] Given the tone of the Portuguese chronicles of the war, mostly written by clerics, Barreto's actions seem singular and strange, but if understood within the long tradition of Portuguese religious relativism and a belief in a shared humanity as well as his own sense of honour, and perhaps self-interest, Barreto's actions may not have been so strange after all.

1   The literature on Dutch toleration is extensive. For a short introduction, see Henry Méchoulan, *Amsterdam au Temps de Spinoza: Argent et Liberté* (Paris 1990). The topic of toleration in Dutch Brazil figures predominantly in studies of that colony, but is virtually absent in the discussions about the general phenomenon in Holland itself. Note for example, its absence in R. Po-Chia Hsia and Henk van Nierop, eds., *Calvinism and Religious Toleration in the Dutch Golden Age* (Cambridge 2002). On Brazil see the summary article by Ronaldo Vainfas, 'La Babel religiosa: Católicos, calvinistas, converses y judíos en Brasil bajo loa domi nación holandesa (1630-54)', in: Jaime Contreras, et al., *Familia, Religion y Negocio* (Madrid 2002) 321-42.

2   This story has now been detailed in Frans Leonard Schalkwijk, *Igreja e Estado no Brasil Holandês* (Recife 1986).

3   For a recent example, see Perez Zagorin, *How the Idea of Religious Toleration came to the West* (Princeton 2003).

4   This point is made by Joachim Whaley, *Religious Toleration and Social Change in Hamburg*, 1529-1819 (Cambridge 1985) 5.

5   The former (exercitium religionis publicum) being reserved for the official religion of the state, and all other religious practice limited to (exercitium religionis privatum) the home or to places of worship that could have no towers, or spires or bells or anything else that would call attention to them. See also Alan Levine, ed., *Early Modern Skepticism and the Origins of Toleration* (Lanham, Md 1999) 1-21.

6   See, for example, Méchoulan, *Amsterdam au Temps de Spinoza*.

7   Ibid., 76.

8   Maria Paula Marçal Lourenço, 'Para o estudos da actividade inquisitorial no Alto Alentejo: a visita da Inquisição de Lisboa ao bispado de Portalegre em 1578-79', *A Cidade*, 3 (1989) 109-38.

9   On 'propositions' see Juan Antonio Alejandre and María Jesús Torquemada, *Palabra de Hereje* (Seville 1998).

10 'Mal hecho el quitar a cada uno el libre albedrio de creer lo que quissiese y obligar a los cristianos a que creyessen por fuerza la ley de Jesu Cristo y le pare ceio mal [...] contra lo que nos enseña la doctrina cristiana'. ADC, Inquisición, leg. 522/6740.

11 AHN, Inq. Lib. 2845 (Murcia).

12 Pareceres sobre se o baptismo salva os hereges que morrem na sua seita, Biblioteca Pública de Évora, CVII/1-26.

13 Werner Thomas, *Los Protestantes y la Inquisición en España en Tiempos de Reforma y Contrarreforma* (Leuven 2001), demonstrates that many persons accused as Protestants by Spanish inquisitorial tribunals also expressed this idea.

14 Arquivo Diocesano de Cuenca, leg. 210, exp. 2419 (1570).

15 Yirmiyahu Yovel, *Spinoza and Other Heretics* (2 vols.; Princeton 1989) I, 159-77. See also Jonathan Israel, *Locke, Spinoza, and the Philosophical Debate Concerning Toleration in the Early Enlightenment* (c. 1670-c.1750) (Amsterdam 1999) 16-17. See also I. S. Révah, *Spinoza and Dr. Juan del Prado* (Paris 1959); Natalia Muchnik, 'Juan de Prado o las peregrinaciones de`un passeur de frontiers', in: Jaime Contreras, et al., *Familia, Religion y Negocio*, 237-68.

16 Francisco Bethencourt, *História das Inquisições* (Lisbon 1994) 311-12, indicates that besides religious policy, Jesuits like Vieira also had convictions that many of the confessions made were invalid.

17 'Se Deus não queria que os n fossem paos porque avião os senhores inquisidores de querer fazer os ditos paos novos paos a força'. Testimony of Domingos Gomes (20 Nov. 1623), ANTT, Inquisição Evora, maço 64, n. 608.

18 ANTT, Inq. Lisboa 202, fol. 645, Caderno do promotor. His trial is found in ANTT, Inq. Lisbon 6789.

19 ANTT, Inq. Lisboa 202 (25 Sept. 1620).

20 See the analysis of the 'Grande Inquirição' of 1646 in Anita Novinsky, *Cristãos Novos na Bahia* (São Paulo 1972) 129-40. She also notes popular resistance to the Inquisition in Brazil in 'A inquisição portugesa a luz de novos estudos', *Revista de la Inquisición* 7 (1998) 297-307.

21 José Antônio Gonsalves de Mello, *Tempo dos Flamengos: Influência da Ocupação Holandesa na Vida e na Cultura do Norte do Brasil* (Rio de Janeiro 1947) 134.

22 Adriaen van der Dussen, *Relatório Sôbre as Capitanias Conquistadas no Brasil Pelos Holandeses* (1639) in: Gonsalves de Mello, *Tempo dos Flamengos*.

23 Anita Novinsky, 'Uma devassa do Bispo Dom Pedro da Silva, 1635-37', *Anais do Museu Paulista*, 22 (1968) 217-85. The original document is in ANTT, Inq. Cadernos do promotor, n. 19.

24 Manuel Calado, *O Valeroso Lucideno* ([1st ed. 1648] 2 vols.; Belo Horizonte 1987). See the discussion in C. R. Boxer, *The Dutch in Brazil 1624-1654* (Oxford 1957) 298-99.

25 Boxer, *The Dutch in Brazil*, 267-69, provides a biography of Moraes, a Brazilian-born Jesuit who changed from Catholic priest to secular Calvinist, married, lived in Leiden for a while, returned to Brazil, and to the Catholic faith. Although his case is particularly colourful, it was not that uncommon for individuals, even clerics, to move back and forth between religions. On New Christians who became Jews and then returned to the Church see, David L. Graizbord, *Souls in Dispute: Converso Identities in Iberia and the Jewish Diaspora* (Philadelphia 2004); Isabel M. R. Mendes Drumond Braga, 'Uma estranha diáspora rumo a Portugal: judeus e cristãos-novos reduzidos à fé católica no século xvii', *Sefarad* 62 (2002) 259-74.

26 Testimony of Francisco Gomes, 256-57.

27 José António Gonsalves de Mello, *João Fernandes Vieira, Mestre-de-Campo do Terço de Infantaria de Pernambuco* (2nd ed., Lisbon 2000) 47-49; Boxer, *The Dutch in Brazil*, 273-76.

28 Gonsalves de Mello, *Tempo dos Flamengos*, 141-43.

29 Bruno Feitler, *Inquisition, Juifs et Nouveaux-Chrétiens au Brésil* (Leuven 2003) 183-85.

30 Johan Maurits was a practicing Calvinist who saw the king of Spain as a primary enemy of the Christian faith and according to his chroniclers he also supposedly held negative opinions about Jews. See Schalkwijk, *Igreja e Estado*, 87. On his measures on behalf of the freedom of conscience of the Portuguese and in defense of their interests see Gaspar Barléu, *História dos Feitos Recentemente Praticados Durante Oito Anos no Brasil* (Belo Horizonte 1974) 53.

31 Johan Maurits's personal negative attitude toward the Jews is suggested in the anti-Semitic remarks of the former Spanish priest turned Calvinist minister Vicente Joaquin Soler. See his correspondence edited by B. N. Teensma, *Dutch Brazil: Vincent Joachim Soler's Seventeen Letters* (Rio de Janeiro 1999) 74. Johan Maurits responded to the intransigence of the Catholic clergy by expelling first the Jesuits and later members of the other missionary orders. These actions and the hostility of some of the Calvinist clergy was used by Mário Neme, *Fórmulas Políticas no Brasil Holandês* (São Paulo 1971) to question the scope and sincerity of Johan Maurits's toleration.

32 Calado, *O Veleroso Lucideno*, I, 165-74.

33 D. Margarida to Cabido da Sé of Miranda (1639) in Schalkwijk, *Igreja e Estado*, 237.

34 This point was made by Portuguese ambassador Francisco de Sousa Coutinho. See Boxer, *The Dutch in Brazil*, 262.

35 Evaldo Cabral de Mello, *Rubro Veio: O Imaginário da Restauração Pernambucana* (2nd ed., Rio de Janeiro 1997); *Olinda Restaurada* (2nd ed., Rio de Janeiro 1998) 381-447.

36 Saul Levy Mortera, 'Providencia de Dios con Ysrael y verdad y eternidad de la ley de Moseh y Nullidad de los demas leyes', (A. Wiznitzer, transl.) *Jewish Social Studies* XVI (1954) 112-13.

Amsterdam Studies in the Dutch Golden Age

Eric Jan Sluijter, *Rembrandt and the Female Nude*
(ISBN 978 90 5356 837 8)

DISSERTATIONS

Erik Swart, *Krijgsvolk. Militaire professionalisering en het ontstaan van het Staatse leger, 1568-1590* (ISBN 9 78 90 5356 876 7)
Griet Vermeesch, *Oorlog, steden en staatsvorming. De grenssteden Gorinchem en Doesburg tijdens de geboorte-eeuw van de Republiek (1570-1680)* (ISBN 978 90 5356 882 8)